DON'T BOTHER ME, I CAN'T COPE

A MUSICAL ENTERTAINMENT
by Micki Grant

Conceived by Vinnette Carroll

SAMUEL FRENCH, INC.
25 WEST 45TH STREET   NEW YORK 10036
7623 SUNSET BOULEVARD   HOLLYWOOD 90046
LONDON   *TORONTO*

Words and Music Copyright ©, 1972,
by Fiddleback Music Publishing Co., Inc.

International Copyright Secured
All Rights Reserved

Amateurs wishing to arrange for the production of DON'T BOTHER ME, I CAN'T COPE must make application to SAMUEL FRENCH, INC., at 25 West 45th Street, New York, N.Y. 10036, giving the following particulars:

(1) The name of the town and theatre or hall in which it is proposed to give the production.

(2) The maximum seating capacity of the theatre or hall.

(3) Scale of ticket prices.

(4) The number of performances it is intended to give, and the dates thereof.

(5) Indicate whether you will use an orchestration or simply a piano.

Upon receipt of these particulars SAMUEL FRENCH, INC., will quote the terms upon which permission for performances will be granted.

A piano conductor score and a set of orchestral parts consisting of drums, guitar, bass & alto sax plus principal chorus books will be loaned two months prior to the production ONLY on receipt of the royalty quoted for all performances, the rental fee and a refundable deposit. The deposit will be refunded on the safe return to SAMUEL FRENCH, INC. of all material loaned for the production.

Stock royalty quoted on application to SAMUEL FRENCH, INC.

For all other rights than those stipulated above, apply to Miss Bertha Case, 42 West 53rd St., New York, N.Y. 10019.

No changes shall be made in the play for the purpose of your production.

ISBN 0 573 68080 9

It will be a part of the conditions of our release of the play for your production that in all programs, billboards, circulars, newspaper advertising or other printed matter under your control, you give authorship credits substantially as follows:

DON'T BOTHER ME, I CAN'T COPE

A Musical Entertainment
by MICKI GRANT

Conceived by
VINNETTE CARROLL

Original Production Directed
by VINNETTE CARROLL

DON'T BOTHER ME, I CAN'T COPE was first presented Apr. 19, 1972 at the Playhouse Theatre, New York City. Produced by Edward Padula and Arch Lustberg, Scenery by Richard A. Miller, Costumes by Edna Watson, Lighting by B. J. Sammler, and Choreographed by George Faison. Conceived and Directed by Vinnette Carroll.

THE COMPANY

ALEX BRADFORD
HOPE CLARKE
MICKI GRANT
BOBBY HILL
ARNOLD WILKERSON

Musicians:

Danny Holgate
 (musical director)
Herb Lovelle—drums
Rudy Stevenson—guitar, flute
Billy Butler—guitar
John Lucien—bass

Dancers:

Thommie Bush
Gerald G. Francis
Ben Harney
Leona Johnson

Singers:

Alberta Bradford
Charles Campbell
Marie Thomas

ACT I

I Gotta Keep Movin'	Alex Bradford, Alberta Bradford, Charles Campbell, Bobby Hill

Danced by *Ben Harney*

Harlem Streets	Dancers
Lookin' Over From Your Side	Bobby Hill
Don't Bother Me, I Can't Cope	Company
When I Feel Like Moving	Hope Clarke and Dancers
Help	Hope Clarke and Dancers
Fighting for Pharaoh	Alex Bradford, Bobby Hill, Alberta Bradford, Charles Campbell
Good Vibrations	Alex Bradford and Company
Love Power	Bobby Hill, Hope Clarke and Company
You Think I Got Rhythm?	Dancers
They Keep Coming	Entire Company
My Name Is Man	Arnold Wilkerson

ACT II

Questions	Micki Grant
It Takes A Whole Lot of Human Feeling	Micki Grant
You Think I Got Rhythm?	Arnold Wilkerson and Micki Grant
Time Brings About A Change	Alex Bradford, Alberta Bradford, Charles Campbell, Micki Grant, Marie Thomas, Arnold Wilkerson
So Little Time	Micki Grant
Thank Heaven For You	Bobby Hill, Micki Grant
So Long Sammy	Bobby Hill

Danced by *Hope Clarke* and *Dancers*

All I Need	Alberta Bradford and Company
I Gotta Keep Movin' (Reprise)	Micki Grant, Alex Bradford and Company

CAST

Consists of six singers and six dancers. Dancers should also be able to sing.

Singers	*Dancers*
SALOME	AGNES
CHARLAINE	JULIA
SHEILA	PAT
CLINTON	EDMUND
NAT	STEVE
TIM	ROBERT

Cast can be augmented or done with as few as nine. See Director's notes.

DON'T BOTHER ME, I CAN'T COPE

ACT ONE

No. 1: I GOTTA KEEP MOVIN'

(EDMUND *is discovered* D. L. *does solo dance through* C.; SALOME *is* U. R. *on stairs.*)

SALOME.
A.
I GOTTA KEEP MOVIN', MOVIN' LORD, I'VE GOTTA KEEP MOVIN', MOVIN' LORD.
I'M A LONG WAY FROM WHERE I'VE BEEN
BUT I GOTTA KEEP MOVIN' TIL' I MOVE ON IN.
B.
I GOTTA KEEP PUSHIN', PUSHIN' LORD, I'VE GOTTA KEEP PUSHIN', PUSHIN' LORD.
I'VE PUSHED A LONG WAY FROM WHERE I'VE BEEN,
BUT I GOTTA KEEP PUSHIN' TIL' I PUSH ON IN.
C.
I GOTTA KEEP RUNNIN', RUNNIN', I'VE GOTTA KEEP RUNNIN' RUNNIN' LORD.
I'VE RUN A LONG WAY FROM WHERE I'VE BEEN
BUT I GOTTA KEEP RUNNIN' TIL' I RUN ON IN.
   (EDMUND *crosses* U. L. *and exits,* SALOME *crosses* D. C.)
D.
I GOTTA KEEP MOVIN'
I GOTTA KEEP MOVIN'
I GOTTA KEEP MOVIN'
I GOTTA KEEP MOVIN' TIL' I MOVE ON IN.
E.
I GOTTA KEEP MOVIN'
I GOTTA KEEP MOVIN'

I GOTTA KEEP MOVIN'
I GOTTA KEEP MOVIN' TIL' I MOVE ON IN.

F.
LIFE'S ROAD IS ROUGH TO TRAVEL } KEEP MOVIN'
NOBODY HAS A MAP } KEEP MOVIN'
BUT I KNOW ONE DAY I'LL FIND A WAY, } UNDER THIS
IF I JUST GO ONE MORE LAP.

    (ROBERT *enters from house* D. L.; *crosses* U. R., *Ex.*)

G.
I GOTTA KEEP MOVIN'
I GOTTA KEEP MOVIN'
I GOTTA KEEP MOVIN'
I GOTTA KEEP MOVIN' TIL' I PUSH ON IN.

    (AGNES *enters same* D. L., *crosses* U. R., *Ex.*)

H.
AT TIMES WHEN I GET DISCOURAGED }
I REMEMBER WHAT I READ ONE DAY, } KEEP MOVIN',
THE RACE IS NOT GIVEN UNTO THE SWIFT, } etc.,
BUT TO HIM THAT ENDURETH ALL THE WAY. } UNDER THIS

    (STEVE *enters same* D. L., *crosses* U. R., *Ext*. CHARLAINE *enters same* D. R., *crosses* L., *Ex.*)

I.
I GOTTA KEEP PUSHIN'
I GOTTA KEEP PUSHIN'
I GOTTA KEEP PUSHIN'
I GOTTA KEEP PUSHIN' TIL' I RUN ON IN.

J.
I GOTTA KEEP MOVIN'
I GOTTA KEEP MOVIN'
I GOTTA KEEP MOVIN'
I GOTTA KEEP MOVIN' TIL' I MOVE ON IN.

    (PAT *enters same* D. L., *crosses* U. R., *Ex. pause*. NAT *enters same* D. R., *crosses* L., *Ex. pause*. ROBERT *enters* D. R., *crosses* U. L., *Ex.*)

K.
I'VE COME THROUGH SOME MIGHTY LOW VALLEYS,
AND OVER MOUNTAINS HARD TO CLIMB

BUT WHEN I LOOK BACK OVER MY TRACKS
IT SEEMS LIKE I'M MARKING TIME.
L.
I GOTTA KEEP MOVIN'
I GOTTA KEEP MOVIN'
I GOTTA KEEP MOVIN'
I GOTTA KEEP RUNNIN' TIL' I MOVE ON IN.
M.
I GOTTA KEEP MOVIN'
I GOTTA KEEP MOVIN'
I GOTTA KEEP MOVIN'
I GOTTA KEEP MOVIN' TIL' I MOVE ON IN.
  CHORUS.
KEEP MOVIN' TIL' I MOVE ON IN
KEEP MOVIN' TIL' I MOVE ON IN
KEEP MOVIN' TIL' I MOVE ON IN.

(SALOME *Ex.* U. L. *Drums into "Harlem" Intro.* PAT *enters* U. R., *crosses* C. AGNES *enters* D. R.)

No. 2: HARLEM STREETS

(*Crosses* D. S. R. *ladder.* STEVE *enters* U. R., *crosses* D. L. ROBERT *enters* U. L., *crosses* U. R. *ladder.* EDMUND *enters* U. L., *crosses* D. L. C. PAT *crosses to* EDMUND *crosses* R.)

PAT.
AIN'T NO WHICH
AIN'T NO WAYS
LIKE THE WHICH-A-WAYS
OF THE HARLEM DAYS.
        (ROBERT *crosses* D. S., AGNES *crosses* D. S.)
  ROBERT.
AIN'T NO SOUNDS
  AGNES.
AIN'T NO SIGHTS
  ROBERT and AGNES.
LIKE THE SIGHTS AND SOUNDS
OF THE HARLEM NIGHTS.
            (EDMUND *spin* D. S.)

EDMUND.
HARLEMESE
AND GEORGIA DRAWL,
                    (STEVE *spin* D. S.)
STEVE.
SWAHILI TOO,
AND THAT AIN'T ALL
ALL.
ON MARCUS GARVEY'S
HOLIDAY
IF YOU AIN'T WEST INDIAN
GET OUT THE WAY.

No. 3: GOIN' TO TOWN THIS MORNING

(JULIA *enters* U. R. *as* "MAVIS," *crosses onto* R. *ladder, crosses around* D. C.)

JULIA.
I played the field in me yesterdays
But now I going to change me ways
So tell the boys when they get hot
Don't come seeking what I got.
                    (JULIA *opens umbrella*.)
LOCK UP THE DOG, PUT OUT THE CAT
GOING TO TOWN THIS MORNING,
DON'T LOOK FOR ME IF I DON'T COME BACK,
GOING TO TOWN THIS MORNING.

LOCK UP THE DOG, PUT OUT THE CAT
GOING TO TOWN THIS MORNING
DON'T LOOK FOR ME IF I DON'T COME BACK
GOING TO TOWN THIS MORNING.
(BOYS *move* C. JULIA *crosses to* ROBERT *and* STEVE. GIRLS *turn* L.)
JULIA.
HEY EVERYBODY, GATHER ROUND,
CHORUS.
GOING TO TOWN THIS MORNING
JULIA.
MAVIS IS GOING TO SETTLE DOWN

ACT I   DON'T BOTHER ME, I CAN'T COPE   11

CHORUS.
GOING TO TOWN THIS MORNING
JULIA.
ME MAN DONE GIVE A RING TO ME
CHORUS.
GOING TO TOWN THIS MORNING
JULIA.
NOW I HIS WOMAN LEGALLY
CHORUS.
GOING TO TOWN THIS MORNING

(EDMUND *crosses to* JULIA; JULIA *straddle* C., *kicks*, EDMUND.)
CHORUS.
SHE MAN DONE GIVE A RING TO SHE (SHOO SHOO SHOO)
NOW SHE HIS WOMAN LEGALLY (SHOO SHOO SHOO)
            (JULIA *sits on* EDMUND.)
JULIA.
NOW SHE ALWAYS MAKING LIKE A SAINT
CHORUS.
GOING TO TOWN THIS MORNING
JULIA.
'CAUSE SHE GOT A RING AND MAVIS AIN'T
CHORUS.
GOING TO TOWN THIS MORNING
        (PAT *crosses* D. S.: JULIA *crosses to* PAT.)
JULIA.
NOW YOU BETTER MIND WHO YOU TALKING TO
CHORUS.
GOING TO TOWN THIS MORNING
JULIA.
'CAUSE NOW I BIG A SAINT AS YOU
CHORUS.
GOING TO TOWN THIS MORNING
    (PAT *chases* JULIA R., *and crosses back to original position.*)
CHORUS.
SHE BETTER MIND WHO SHE TALKING TO (SHOO SHOO SHOO)
'CAUSE NOW SHE BIG A SAINT AS YOU (SHOO SHOO SHOO)
            (NAT *crosses to* JULIA D. R.)

NAT.
I VERY HAPPILY SURPRISED
　CHORUS.
GOING TO TOWN THIS MORNING
　NAT.
YOU GOT YOUR LOVING LEGALIZED
　CHORUS.
GOING TO TOWN THIS MORNING
　NAT.
BUT GIRL I GOT JUST ONE COMPLAINT
　CHORUS.
GOING TO TOWN THIS MORNING
　NAT.
ENGAGED YOU IS BUT SAINT YOU AIN'T.
　CHORUS.
GOING TO TOWN THIS MORNING
　　　　　(NAT *and* JULIA *crosses* C.)
　CHORUS.
LOCK UP THE DOG, PUT OUT THE CAT
GOING TO TOWN THIS MORNING
DON'T LOOK FOR ME IF I DON'T COME BACK
GOING TO TOWN THIS MORNING

(JULIA *pushes* NAT *down with umbrella.* NAT *crosses* U. S. L. *ladder.*)

　JULIA.
NOBODY GONNA HAVE MAVIS
　CHORUS.
GOING TO TOWN THIS MORNING
　JULIA.
EXCEPT THE MAN WHO GAVE ME THIS
　CHORUS.
GOING TO TOWN THIS MORNING

(*DANCE SEQUENCE. Limbo*—STEVE *and* ROBERT *mime pole* R. *of* L. *ladder.* JULIA *limbos to pole.* NAT *limbos* D. S. *to* JULIA; JULIA *slaps* NAT; *he crosses* L. *ladder.* EDMUND *crosses* U. S. *of limbo and pulls* JULIA *under;* BOTH *cross* C. JULIA *mounts* EDMUND'S *shoulders.* NAT *hands umbrella to* ROBERT; ROBERT *opens it and hands it to* JULIA.)

CHORUS.
LOCK UP THE DOG, PUT OUT THE CAT
GOING TO TOWN THIS MORNING
DON'T LOOK FOR ME IF I DON'T COME BACK
GOING TO TOWN THIS MORNING
LOCK UP THE DOG, PUT OUT THE CAT
GOING TO TOWN THIS MORNING
DON'T LOOK FOR ME IF I DON'T COME BACK
GOING TO TOWN THIS MORNING
GOING TO TOWN THIS MORNING
GOING TO TOWN THIS MORNING.
(JULIA *and* EDMUND *exit* U. R.)

No. 4: HARLEM STREETS

(PAT *crosses* D. L.)

PAT.
AIN'T NO WHICH
AIN'T NO WAYS
LIKE THE WHICH-A-WAYS
OF THE HARLEM DAYS.
(NAT *crosses* L.)

NAT.
AIN'T NO SOUNDS
AIN'T NO SIGHTS
LIKE THE SIGHTS AND SOUNDS
OF THE HARLEM NIGHTS.
(NAT *crosses* D. S.)

No. 5: LOOKING OVER FROM YOUR SIDE

(CLINTON *the "preacher" in Act II standing on* L. S. *ladder till* "Rats were having a party in the hall" *then crosses* C. S. *using ladder as a fire escape.*)

CLINTON.
LAST NIGHT LEFT ME TIRED
I HARDLY SLEPT AT ALL

'CAUSE THE RATS WERE HAVIN'
A PARTY IN THE HALL.
    (CLINTON *crosses* R. C.)
THE CITY JUST DECIDED
TO CONDEMN THIS TENEMENT.
THAT'S WHEN THE LANDLORD DECIDED
HE WAS GONNA RAISE THE RENT.

LOOKIN' OVER FROM YOUR SIDE,
THINGS MAY LOOK REAL FINE.
BUT IF YOU WERE LOOKIN' FROM MY SIDE,
I BET YOU'D CHANGE YOUR MIND.
    (CLINTON *crosses* R.)
I CAN'T EVEN SLEEP
IN MY OWN HARD-EARNED BED
'CAUSE THE PLASTER FROM THE CEILING
KEEPS FALLIN' ON MY HEAD.
BUT YOU SAY THIS HOUSE IS QUAINT.
IT'S SO OLD IT'S FILLED WITH HISTORY.
IT MAY BE QUAINT TO YOU,
BUT IT'S JUST A BIG HEADACHE FOR ME.
    (CLINTON *crosses* U. C. *to* R. *ladder*.)
LOOKIN' OVER FROM YOUR SIDE,
YOU SAY, "COMPLAININ' AGAIN? WHAT'S NEW?"
BUT IF YOU WERE LOOKIN' FROM MY SIDE,
YOU'D BE COMPLAININ' TOO.
    (CLINTON *crosses* C.)
THE WINDOW PANE IS BROKEN
AND WINTER'S COMIN' IN,
AND I'M GETTIN' TIRED OF SCRAPIN'
JACK FROST OFF MY SKIN,
BUT YOU SAY "THAT BREEZE FEELS GOOD,"
AS YOU TURN YOUR THERMOSTAT TO EIGHTY-THREE.
WELL, WHAT FEELS GOOD TO YOU
FEELS LIKE PNEUMONIA TO ME.
    (CLINTON *crosses* D. S.)
LOOKIN' OVER FROM YOUR SIDE,
IT'S ALL PEACE AND QUIET,
BUT IF YOU WERE LOOKIN' FROM MY SIDE,
YOU MIGHT EVEN START A RIOT.
    (CLINTON *crosses* U. R. *ladder, sits*.)

LOOKIN' OVER FROM YOUR SIDE,
IT'S ALL PEACE AND QUIET.
BUT IF YOU WERE LOOKIN' FROM MY SIDE
YOU MIGHT EVEN START A . . . RIOT.

No. 6: DON'T BOTHER ME, I CAN'T COPE

(PAT *crosses* D. S.—X. L.)

PAT.
I lay back on my analyst's couch
And told him what's frustrating me.
He said, "The trouble with you is you can't cope,"
Then he asked me for a fifty dollar fee.

I said, "Don't bother me, I can't cope.
Do you think I'm paying you that kind of dough
For telling me something I already know?
That's why I'm here, fool, 'cause I can't cope!"

CHORUS.
SHE SAID DON'T BOTHER HER,
SHE CAN'T COPE.

(CHARLAINE *crosses* L. C.)

CHARLAINE.
I was on my first trip in a jet plane
To see some folks in Atlanta
VOICE.
Yeah?
CHARLAINE.
When a voice said, "Fasten your seat belts, please,
We're about to land in Havana."
VOICE.
Wooooooooo-o!
CHARLAINE.
I screamed, "Don't bother me, I can't cope!
I don't care if we are aloft,
Stop this thing and let me off.
No habla espanol baby,
And I can't cope."

CHORUS.
SHE SAID DON'T BOTHER HER,
SHE CAN'T COPE.
   TIM.
I chauffeured my boss around all day
And after I dropped off the car
I stopped in to do some relaxing
At the neighborhood bar
And this tall, fine, painted lady
Sat down on the next stool.
She said, "How ya doin', sweet daddy?"
Now you're gonna think I'm a fool
'Cause I said, "I ain't doin'
And that's no joke
Your shape is divine
And your talk is sweet
But my motor's run down
And I'm dead on my feet.
I been ridin' all day, and I can't cope!"
   CHORUS.
HE SAID DON'T BOTHER HIM,
HE CAN'T COPE.
                    (STEVE *crosses* C.)
   STEVE.
The landlord sold my building
Without asking my consent
And my brand-new landlord told me
To vacate or pay more rent.
I said, "Man, do you think
I'm some kind of dope?
This place ain't fit for occupancy
The way I see it, you owe me!
Now get out of my doorway
'Cause I can't cope!"
   CHORUS.
HE SAID DON'T BOTHER HIM,
HE CAN'T COPE.
   STEVE.
Anybody know where I can find a nice room?
              (JULIA *crosses* D. R. *to* EDMUND.)

ACT I   DON'T BOTHER ME, I CAN'T COPE   17

JULIA. (*With West Indian accent.*)
I went to the unemployment office
To sign my weekly card,
And the clerk had the nerve to ask me
If I had looked for work real hard.
I said, "Don't vex me, madam, I can't cope.
And smile a little when you speak
'Cause you may be on this line yourself next week,
Not put me money where your mouth is,
'Cause I can't cope."
    CHORUS.
SHE SAID DON'T BOTHER HER,
SHE CAN'T COPE.
    CLINTON.
When I asked my boss for a raise in pay,
He shook his head and replied, "No way!"
I must refuse for the good of the nation,
We're in a recession and a raise is inflation."
I said, "Cut the double talk, man, I can't cope.
But you've made a good point, I must confess,
My appetite's inflated and my stomach's recessed,
So guess who's coming to dinner,
'Cause I can't cope."
    CHORUS.
HE SAID DON'T BOTHER HIM,
HE CAN'T COPE.
    SHEILA.
My boss lady was smiling
When she said, "Now listen, Ella Mae,
You're not giving me a full day's work
Why, you took two coffee breaks today."
I smiled back, "That's right, sugah,
It helps me cope,
And I also . . .
Did four laundry loads
And ironed it too.
Ran the vacuum, washed the blinds,
Top-Jobbed the floor and cooked a stew,
Then—took Junior to the playground,
But I don't blame you a bit
And tomorrow I'll do better

Because today I quit!
Go find yourself another workhorse,
'Cause I can't cope!"

CHORUS.
SHE SAID DON'T BOTHER HER,
SHE CAN'T COPE.

PAT.
I RETURNED TO MY ANALYST'S COUCH
STILL LOOKING FOR SOME PEACE OF MIND
AND I COULD TELL BY THE LOOK ON HIS FACE
THAT HIS JOB WAS BECOMING A GRIND.

NAT.
"NOT YOU AGAIN!" HE MOANED. "I CAN'T COPE.
I KNOW YOU'VE GOT TROUBLES BUT I'VE GOT A FEW
SO LET ME LIE ON THAT COUCH
AND TALK TO YOU.

IN THE CITY WE NEVER WENT OUT AFTER DARK
WE HAD THREE CARS BETWEEN US BUT NO PLACE TO PARK
SO WE STARTED COMMUTING AND THEY RAISED ALL THE TOLLS
NOW THEY WANT TO PLUG UP MY TAX LOOPHOLES.
MY SON'S SMOKING POT
AND WHEN I ASKED HIM WHY
HE SAID "POT OR MARTINIS, PA,
WE'RE BOTH GETTING HIGH."
MY DAUGHTER ANNOUNCED
THAT I HAD A GRANDSON
WHEN I ASKED WHERE'S THE FATHER
SHE SAID, "WHO NEEDS ONE?"
NOW MY WIFE'S LIBERATED
AND THE HOUSE HAS TWO HEADS
SO WE EAT OUT EVERY NIGHT
AND SHE'S ORDERED TWIN BEDS.

PAT.
I SAID HOLD IT BROTHER, I CAN'T COPE.
YOUR RECITATION HAS REDUCED ME TO TEARS
YOU'VE GOT ENOUGH PROBLEMS
TO LAST YOU FOR YEARS
BETWEEN YOURS AND MINE

ACT I DON'T BOTHER ME, I CAN'T COPE 19

IT'S HARD TO KEEP TRACK
BUT I'M STILL ONE UP ON YOU.
YOU AIN'T BLACK
BUT—
  COMPANY.
YOU GOTTA COPE
I GOTTA COPE
ALL GOD'S CHILLUN GOTTA COPE.
                    (*Drumbeat.*)

No. 7: CHILDREN'S RHYMES

  CHORUS.
CZECHOSLOVAKIA   BUM MIDI BUM
YUGOSLAVIA   BUM MIDI BUM

      (SALOME *enters* R., *joins* NAT *and* CHARLAINE R. *of* C.)

LET'S GET THE RHYTHM OF THE HANDS
  CHORUS.
WE GOT THE RHYTHM OF THE HANDS
              (NAT *crosses* D. C.)
  NAT.
HAM-BONE HAM-BONE WHERE'VE YOU BEEN
ROUND THE CORNER AND BACK AGAIN

HAM-BONE HAM-BONE WHERE'S YOUR WIFE
IN THE KITCHEN COOKIN' RICE
HAM-BONE HAM-BONE HAM-BONE HAM-BONE
              (SALOME *crosses* C.)
  SALOME.
LET'S GET THE RHYTHM OF THE HIPS
     (JULIA *crosses* C., *chase* NAT, SALOME, CHARLAINE *off* R.)
  GIRL DANCERS.
WE GOT THE RHYTHM OF THE HIPS
                 (DANCERS *move cross* S.)
LET'S GET THE RHYTHM OF THE HEAD
          (STEVE *crosses from* R. *of* C., *wiggles head*.)
  STEVE.
WE GOT THE RHYTHM OF THE HEAD
LET'S GET THE RHYTHM OF THE FEET

DANCERS.
WE GOT THE RHYTHM OF THE FEET
DA, DA, DA DA DA
DA, DA, DA DA DA

(PAT *crosses* D. C.)

PAT.
WHEN I FEEL IKE MOVIN'
DON'T WANT SHOES
ALL I WANT IS SOME
LOW-DOWN BLUES.

BLACK BOTTOM, CHARLESTON,
BOOGALOO,
JITTERBUG, BUMP
AND THE HUSTLE, TOO.

SAVOY STOMPERS
STOMPIN' TIL' DAWN
COTTON CLUB CUTIES
CARRYIN' ON.

SMALL'S PARADISE
OR MADISON SQUARE
WHEN I FEEL LIKE MOVIN'
I DON'T CARE.

No. 8: HISTORY OF DANCE

(Slow Blues. Dance—Guitar, Drums.)

(This sequence is the history of the dance from the Charleston to the Hustle. The choreographer has the option to end the sequence with the current popular dance craze.)

(Top of Charleston, end of Charleston,
 End of break [blues music];
 Top of Jitterbug,
 Top of acid rock,
 Middle of acid rock, (music change)
 End of acid rock.

(*BILLIE HOLIDAY music, spotlight on* SHEILA U. L.)

No. 9: BILLIE HOLIDAY BLUES

(SHEILA U. L., NAT *and* SALOME *enter* U. R. TIM *leans against ladder.*)

SHEILA.
DADDY WAS A BOY AND MAMMA SHE WAS JUST A GIRL
DADDY WAS A BOY AND MAMMA SHE WAS JUST A GIRL
WHEN THEY BOTH GOT TOGETHER
AND BROUGHT YOU INTO THIS OLD WORLD

A WEED GROWS BY ITSELF
A CACTUS GROWS IN SAND
BILLIE HOLIDAY
JUST GROWS THE BEST WAY THAT SHE CAN
ANYTHING WORTH KNOWIN'
YOU KNEW IT ALL BY TEN
WHERE SOME FOLKS ARE STILL GOIN'
IS ALREADY WHERE YOU'VE BEEN

IT TAKES A LOT MORE THAN JUST TRYIN'
IT TAKES A WHOLE LOT MORE TO WIN
IT TAKES A LOT MORE THAN JUST TRYIN'
IT TAKES A WHOLE LOT MORE TO WIN
WHEN THE WORLD CAN'T SEE BEYOND
THE DARK BROWN WRAPPER THAT YOU'RE IN

(*The following is optional. Orchestra must ad lib.*)

SOME FOLKS CALL YOU BILLIE
SOME SAY LADY IS YOUR NAME
IT DON'T MATTER WHAT THEY CALL YOU
WHEN THEY ALL TREAT YOU THE SAME
    (CLINTON *enters* R., *crosses* U. S. *of* R. *ladder.*)
SOME KIND OF LIVIN' BEATS ANY KIND OF DYIN'
YES . . . SOME KIND OF LIVIN' BEATS ANY KIND OF DYIN'
AND SINGIN' WHEN YOUR HEART ACHES
SURE BEATS THE HELL OUT OF CRYIN'
    (SHEILA *Ex.* U. L.)

No. 10: GHETTO LIFE

(*During following song,* AGNES *crosses to* ROBERT *on* L. *ladder;* EDMUND *crosses* U. S. *of* L. *ladder;* ROBERT *crosses* D. S.; STEVE *puts money on* JULIA'S *dress.* JULIA *and* STEVE *split;* JULIA *crosses* C. *to* ROBERT, *who slaps her, takes money and throws it into the pit.* JULIA *and* ROBERT *cross* U. C., JULIA *Ex.* U. R. TIM *remains against ladder.*)

CHORUS.
The pimp pimpin', the hooker hookin'

The pusher pushin', Adam's gone
And ghetto life goes on and on and on and on . . .

The trippers trippin', the tryers tryin',
The younguns dyin', a new one's born
And ghetto life goes on and on and on and on . . .

Another team of astronauts went to the moon
Agnew went to court, Kissinger went to and fro

Nixon went to China
While Bobby Lee Jones went to Viet Nam
Now he's gone and ghetto life goes on and on and on and on . . .
  (JULIA *enters* U. R., *crosses* D. L. *to* EDMUND.)
With the takers takin',
The hopeful hopin',
The faithful prayin',
The copers copin',
Comes the dawn
And ghetto life goes on and on and on and on and on and on
And on and on and on . . .
(STEVE *Ex.* R. SALOME *crosses* R.: AGNES *Ex.* L., JULIA *Ex.* L. TIM *goes up* R. *ladder.*)

No. 11: YOU THINK I GOT RHYTHM

   (NAT *crosses* L.)
NAT.
AIN'T NO JOY, AIN'T NO STRIFE
LIKE THE JOY AND THE STRIFE OF GHETTO LIFE.
   (EDMUND *crosses* U. C.)
EDMUND.
PLAY THOSE DRUMS

PLAY 'EM HOT.
YOU THINK I'VE GOT RHYTHM?
GOT A LOT.

(EDMUND *dances; ends up* R. *of* C. CHARLAINE *enters* L., *crosses* D. S. *of* L. *ladder*.)

CHARLAINE.
HIT THOSE KEYS
LOUD AND LONG.
YOU THINK I CAN SING THE BLUES?
YOU'RE NOT WRONG.

YOU CAN'T BE DISAPPOINTED
WHEN YOU'RE DISAPPOINTED ALL THE TIME.
NO, YOU CAN'T BE DISAPPOINTED
WHEN YOU'RE DISAPPOINTED ALL THE TIME.
EVERY TIME I MAKE A DOLLAR
IT ENDS UP LOOKING LIKE A DIME.
  (*Drums*.)
TURN THAT JUKE BOX
WAY UP HIGH,
YOU THINK WE LIKE A GOOD TIME?
NO LIE.

(EDMUND *and* CHARLAINE *meet* C. S., *turn*. CHARLAINE R., EDMUND *crosses* L. C. S., *faces* U. S.)

EDMUND.
SEE THAT BACK?
SEE THAT HAND?
YOU THINK I CAN TOTE A BARGE?
WELL, I CAN.

AND LEAD MILLIONS IN PEACE,
AND DISCOVER BLOOD PLASMA
  (EDMUND *and* CHARLAINE *takes hands*.)
CHARLAINE.
AND CONDUCT SYMPHONY ORCHESTRAS
EDMUND.
AND MAKE IT TO THE NORTH POLE

} No Music

(EDMUND *and* CHARLAINE *cross* U. C., *stop and turn on* "*Oh*".)

EDMUND and CHARLAINE.
OH . . . AND PICK COTTON.

No. 12: TIME BRINGS ABOUT A CHANGE

(ROBERT *Ex.* L.; NAT *Ex.* R., STEVE *and* PAT *enter* R.; JULIA *enters* L.; CHARLAINE *and* EDMUND *cross* D. C. *Between verses, all dance a soft shoe with arms front as if holding a cane. On chorus, all dance in a line* D. C. *On verse, all pose with hands at faces, a la minstrel except the speaker, whose arms are front.*)

CHORUS.
TIME BRINGS ABOUT A CHANGE,
TIME BRINGS ABOUT A CHANGE,
TIME BRINGS ABOUT A CHANGE,
TIME WILL BRING A CHANGE ABOUT.

TIME BRINGS ABOUT A CHANGE,
TIME BRINGS ABOUT A CHANGE,
TIME BRINGS ABOUT A CHANGE,
TIME WILL BRING A CHANGE ABOUT.

CLINTON.
#1.
WHEN I WAS A LAD OF TEN
IN WEATHER HOT OR COOL,
THE WHITE KIDS RODE ON A BIG YELLOW BUS,
WHILE I WALKED NINE MILES TO SCHOOL.
(*Sings.*)
TIME BRINGS ABOUT A CHANGE
TIME WILL BRING A CHANGE ABOUT
TIME BRINGS ABOUT A CHANGE
TIME WILL BRING A CHANGE ABOUT.

JULIA.
#2.
TODAY WHITE FOLKS HAVE CHANGED THEIR MINDS
AND SO THEY FUSS AND CUSS,
BECAUSE NOW THEY WANT TO WALK TO SCHOOL,
AND LEAVE THE DRIVING TO US.
(*Sings.*)
TIME BRINGS ABOUT A CHANGE,
TIME BRINGS ABOUT A CHANGE,
TIME BRINGS ABOUT A CHANGE
TIME WILL BRING A CHANGE ABOUT.

ACT I   DON'T BOTHER ME, I CAN'T COPE

STEVE.
#3.
WHEN I WAS A LAD OF TWELVE
AND BLACKS WERE STILL NEGROES,
A LITTLE WHITE BOY CALLED ME BLACK,
AND I PUNCHED HIM IN THE NOSE.
   (*Sings.*)
TIME BRINGS ABOUT A CHANGE
TIME WILL BRING A CHANGE ABOUT
TIME BRINGS ABOUT A CHANGE
TIME WILL BRING A CHANGE ABOUT.

CHARLAINE.
#4.
MY LITTLE BROTHER CAME HOME TODAY,
HIS FACE ALL IN A POUT.
HE SAID, "SOME KID CALLED ME A NEGRO,
AND I PUNCHED HIM IN THE MOUTH."
   (*Sings.*)
TIME BRINGS ABOUT A CHANGE,
TIME BRINGS ABOUT A CHANGE,
TIME BRINGS ABOUT A CHANGE,
TIME WILL BRING A CHANGE ABOUT.

STEVE.
#5.
Y'ALL REMEMBER BEULAH?
(STEVE *breaks, crosses* D. S.; ALL *drop hands in "shock."* STEVE *does embarrassed take crosses* U. S., *poses. At end of next line* ALL *hands go back to original position*.)
SHE WAS SUCH A CARICATURE
AND "AMOS 'N' ANDY" MADE ME MAD,
THEY WERE STEREOTYPES FOR SURE.
   (*Sings.*)
TIME BRINGS ABOUT A CHANGE
TIME WILL BRING A CHANGE ABOUT
TIME BRINGS ABOUT A CHANGE
TIME WILL BRING A CHANGE ABOUT.

PAT.
#6.
BUT THEY'VE STOPPED ALL THAT OFFENSIVE STUFF
DARKIES CROONING "OH, SUSANNAH"

WE'VE GOT "ARCHIE BUNKER" NOW,
AND THAT'S PURE AMERICANA.
  (*Sings.*)
TIME BRINGS ABOUT A CHANGE
TIME BRINGS ABOUT A CHANGE
TIME BRINGS ABOUT A CHANGE
TIME WILL BRING A CHANGE ABOUT.
  JULIA.
#7.
SOMEBODY STARTED A RUMOR THAT
SOCIALIZING WITH BLACKS COULD BE FUN,
AND PRETTY SOON, AS THE WORD GOT 'ROUND,
EVERY COCKTAIL PARTY HAD ONE.
  (*Sings.*)
TIME BRINGS ABOUT A CHANGE
TIME WILL BRING A CHANGE ABOUT
TIME BRINGS ABOUT A CHANGE
TIME WILL BRING A CHANGE ABOUT
  CLINTON.
#8.
NOW ALL THE GOOD WHITE FOLKS HAVE GONE AND LEFT TOWN,
FOR IT WASN'T FUN ANY MORE,
WHEN THOSE FUN COLORED FOLK LEFT THE COCKTAIL PARTY
AND BOUGHT THE HOUSE NEXT DOOR.
  CHORUS.
TIME BRINGS ABOUT A CHANGE,
TIME BRINGS ABOUT A CHANGE,
TIME BRINGS ABOUT A CHANGE,
TIME WILL BRING A CHANGE ABOUT.

(ALL *gives Black Power salute. This changes into the peace sign. Arms drop slowly.*)

No. 13: SO LITTLE TIME

(SALOME *enters* D. R. *to* R. *of* C.; STEVE, PAT, CHARLAINE *kneel* R.; CLINTON *and* JULIA *cross* L., *face* R.)
  SALOME.

I'VE GOT NO TIME FOR HATING, NO TIME.
THE RIVER ROLLS, AND SO DOES TIME.

LOVING COMES EASY ONCE YOU START,
BUT HATING JUST TAKES TOO MUCH HEART.
THE RIVER'S ROLLIN' AND THERE'S SO LITTLE TIME,
THERE'S SO LITTLE TIME.
            (SALOME *crosses* C.)
I'VE GOT NO TIME FOR NAME CALLING, NO TIME.
THE RIVER ROLLS, AND SO DOES TIME.
BUT OF ALL THE NAMES THAT I COULD CALL,
TO CALL A MAN "BROTHER" IS BEST OF ALL.
THE RIVER'S ROLLIN' AND THERE'S SO LITTLE TIME,
THERE'S SO LITTLE TIME.

SO LITTLE TIME FOR TOUCHING HANDS
SO LITTLE TIME FOR TAKING STANDS
PLENTY OF LIFE STILL IN THE CUP
SO LITTLE TIME TO DRINK IT UP.

I'VE GOT NO TIME FOR KILLING, NO TIME.
THE RIVER ROLLS, AND SO DOES TIME.
THOUGH A MAN MAY BE MY ENEMY,
WHEN I MURDER HIM, I MURDER ME.
THE RIVER'S ROLLIN' AND THERE'S SO LITTLE TIME.
THERE'S SO LITTLE TIME.

  SALOME and CHORUS.
SO LITTLE TIME FOR MAKING FRIENDS
SO LITTLE TIME FOR REACHING ENDS
PLENTY OF LIFE STILL IN THE CUP
SO LITTLE TIME TO DRINK IT UP.
JUST TIME TO KNOW MY FELLOW MAN
AND LEAVE SOME FOOTPRINTS IN THE SAND.
PLENTY OF LIFE STILL IN THE CUP.
SO LITTLE TIME TO DRINK IT UP . . .
  SALOME.
SO LITTLE TIME.
            (SALOME *Ex*. R. STEVE *and* PAT *Ex*. R.)

No. 14: THANK HEAVEN

(NAT *enters* D. L.)
  NAT.
WHEN I'M WORRIED, JUST A SMILE FROM YOU IS ALL
  I NEED.

WHEN I'M FAILING, JUST A WORD FROM YOU AND
I'LL SUCCEED.
WHEN I DON'T HAVE A CENT TO MY NAME I'M STILL
RICH INDEED
  (JULIA *and* KIM *exit* D. L.; PAT *and* STEVE *exit* D. R.)
'CAUSE I'VE GOT YOU AND YOUR LOVE TO GUIDE ME,
  (CHARLAINE *crosses* C.; NAT *crosses to her.*)
YOU TO LIE BESIDE ME,
WITHOUT YOU, I DON'T KNOW WHAT I'D DO,
THANK HEAVEN FOR YOU.
  CHARLAINE.
WHEN I'M TIRED, YOU CAN TOUCH MY BROW AND
I'M AS GOOD AS NEW.
AND WHEN TROUBLES MULTIPLY YOU MAKE THEM
SEEM SO FEW.
AND SOMEHOW YOU MAKE ME BELIEVE THERE'S
NOTHIN' I CAN'T DO,
'CAUSE I'VE GOT YOU AND YOUR LOVE TO GUIDE ME
YOU TO LIE BESIDE ME,
WITHOUT YOU I DON'T KNOW WHAT I'D DO,
THANK HEAVEN FOR YOU.
  NAT *and* CHARLAINE.
BEFORE YOU CAME ALONG, EVERYTHING WENT
WRONG,
AND IT DIDN'T TAKE MUCH TO MAKE A MESS OF ME.
BUT NOW I'M STEPPING HIGH, MY HEAD'S IN THE SKY,
AND NOTHING CAN GET THE BEST OF ME,
'CAUSE I'VE GOT YOU AND YOUR LOVE TO GUIDE ME
YOU TO LIE BESIDE ME,
WITHOUT YOU, I DON'T KNOW WHAT I'D DO,
THANK HEAVEN FOR YOU.
THANK HEAVEN FOR YOU.
THANK HEAVEN FOR YOU.
THANK HEAVEN FOR YOU.
THANK HEAVEN FOR YOU.

  (CHARLAINE *and* NAT *spin out. She crosses up on* R. *ladder;* NAT
  crosses up on L. *ladder.*)

BEFORE YOU CAME ALONG, EVERYTHING WENT
WRONG.

AND IT DIDN'T TAKE MUCH TO MAKE A MESS OF ME.
BUT NOW I'M STEPPING HIGH, MY HEAD'S IN THE SKY,
AND NOTHING CAN GET THE BEST OF ME.
(NAT *and* CHARLAINE *cross* C.)
'CAUSE I'VE GOT YOU AND YOUR LOVE TO GUIDE ME
YOU TO LIE BESIDE ME
WITHOUT YOU I DON'T KNOW WHAT I'D DO
THANK HEAVEN FOR YOU.
THANK HEAVEN FOR YOU.
THANK HEAVEN FOR YOU.
THANK HEAVEN FOR YOU.
THANK HEAVEN FOR YOU.

(CHARLAINE *and* NAT *kiss and dance* U. S. C., *as the* **THREE WOMAN'S LIB GIRLS** *enter and "break up" their dance;* THEY *dance* U. S. C., *and freeze.*)

No. 15: SHOW ME THAT SPECIAL GENE

(JULIA *enters* U. R., *crosses* U. C.; AGNES *enters* D. R., PAT *enters* D. L.; JULIA *crosses* C., *divides* CHARLAINE *and* NAT, *then crosses* U. C., *and dances.* GIRLS *join* D. C.)

GIRLS.
GOD MADE EVELYN FOR ADAM (*Pronounced Eve-lyn.*)
TO KEEP THE MAN COMPANY
HE SAID, "YOU'VE GOT
THE RUN OF THE GARDEN,
JUST STAY AWAY FROM THAT TREE."
 AGNES.
NOW DON'T YOU KNOW
EVELYN BIT ON THE APPLE
AND THAT MAN WAS NOT HARD TO CONVINCE
SO THEY BOTH WERE EQUALLY SINFUL,
 ALL. (*Sing.*)
BUT THEY AIN'T BEEN EQUAL SINCE.
(GIRLS DANCE C.)
 GIRLS.
SHOW ME THAT SPECIAL GENE THAT SAYS
I WAS BORN TO MAKE THE BEDS.

SHOW ME THAT CERTAIN CHROMOSOME
THAT SAYS MY PLACE IS IN THE HOME.
    Pat. (*She crosses* L.)
A MAN THINKS THAT WASHING THE DISHES
IS SOMETHING A WOMAN ADORES,
AND JUST BECAUSE SHE'S A FEMALE
SHE CAN'T WAIT TO SCRUB THE FLOORS.

A MAN THINKS THAT HANGING HIS BRITCHES
IS A CHORE HIS WIFE LOVES TO DO.
AND BECAUSE SHE LOVES THEIR NEW BABY,
SHE LOVES CHANGING DIAPERS TOO.
    Girls. (*They dance* L.)
SHOW ME THAT SPECIAL GENE THAT SAYS
I WAS BORN TO MAKE THE BEDS.   (TWO, THREE, FOUR)
SHOW ME THAT CERTAIN CHROMOSOME
THAT SAYS MY PLACE IS IN THE HOME.
    (Julia *crosses* L. *ladder*.)
    Julia.
A MAN THINKS IT'S PERFECTLY NAT'RAL
TO LEAVE THE HOUSE EVERY DAY,
AND WORK ALONGSIDE SOME WOMAN
WHO'S GETTING UNEQUAL PAY.

THE BOSS EXPECTS THAT SAME WOMAN
TO USE ALL HER INTELLIGENCE,
BUT THE BOSS NEVER THINKS OF PAYING
EQUAL PAY FOR EQUAL SENSE.
    Girls. (*They slow kick*.)
SHOW ME THAT SPECIAL GENE THAT SAYS
I WAS BORN TO MAKE THE BEDS.
SHOW ME THAT CERTAIN CHROMOSOME
THAT SAYS MY PLACE IS IN THE HOME.
    Pat. (*Spoken*.)
I CAN DRIVE A STATION WAGON
BUT I CAN'T DRIVE A TRAIN.
    Julia.
I CAN USE MY BODY,
BUT GOD FORBID MY BRAIN.

PAT.
I CAN TURN A MATTRESS,
OR HAUL THE TRASH OUT BACK,
  JULIA.
I CAN CART THE GROCERIES
BUT NOT A GARMENT RACK.
  PAT. (*She crosses upon* R. *ladder*.)
BETTY FRIEDAN, GERMAINE GREER
ALL TOGETHER NOW,
  GIRLS.
HEAR! HEAR! HEAR!
GLORIA STEINMAN, FLORENCE KENNEDY,
SUSAN B. ANTHONY
AND *ME!*
  GIRLS. (*They join* C., *and dance*.)
SHOW ME THAT SPECIAL GENE THAT SAYS
I WAS BORN TO MAKE THE BEDS.   (TWO, THREE,
                                                 FOUR)
SHOW ME THAT CERTAIN CHROMOSOME
THAT SAYS MY PLACE IS IN THE HOME.
              (CHARLAINE *crosses* D. S., NAT *follows*.)
  GIRLS.
MY PLACE IS IN THE HOME
MY PLACE IS IN THE HOME
MY PLACE IS IN THE HOME
MY PLACE IS IN THE HOME.
  CHARLAINE and NAT.
HOME, HOME ON THE RANGE
          (NAT *lifts* CHARLAINE *in arms, turns* U. S.)
  CHARLAINE.
THERE'S NO PLACE LIKE HOME.
              (NAT *moves* U. S.)
MY PLACE IS IN THE HOME.
MY PLACE IS IN THE HOME.
MY PLACE IS IN THE HOME.
     (NAT *deposits* CHARLAINE U. S.; *kisses her and exits* R.)
THERE'S NO PLACE LIKE HOME
MY PLACE IS IN THE HOME
MY PLACE IS IN THE HOME
MY PLACE IS IN THE HOME.

GIRLS. (*They cross* R. *Spoken mockingly and sassily.*)
Kissy, kissy, kissy.
Show her the way to go home.
Show her the way to go home.

(CHARLAINE *crosses to* U. S. C., *kneels in praying position as her "master" departs.* SHEILA *dances in from* U. S. L., *and between the two factions. She begins singing* D. S. R. *and then works around* S. L. *ladder as she gets more involved in song.*)

No. 16: MY LOVE'S SO GOOD

SHEILA.
ANYTIME I'M FEELING BLUE THE ONLY THING I HAVE TO DO IS THINK OF HIM
AND WHEN I'M THROUGH MY BLUES ARE GONE.
JUST THE MEMORY OF LAST NIGHT CAN GET THE MORNING STARTED RIGHT
AND KEEP MY EVERY HOUR BRIGHT FROM DAWN TO DAWN,
AND THE THOUGHT OF HAVING MORE OF WHAT I HAD THE NIGHT BEFORE CAN
MAKE MY SPIRITS SOAR ABOVE THE HIGHEST CLOUD,
THEN THE THOUGHT OF MY GOOD FORTUNE OVERTAKES ME AND IT MAKES ME FEEL SO PROUD.

MY LOVE'S SO GOOD. MY LOVE'S SO FINE.
HE MAKES ME FEEL SO GOOD. SO GLAD HE'S MINE.

WHEN I WALK ALONG THE STREET I WANT TO STOP THE FOLKS I MEET
AND TELL THEM JUST HOW SWEET MY LOVE HAS BEEN TO ME
WHEN I HEAR THE CHIRPING BIRDS I WANT TO FILL THEIR MOUTHS WITH WORDS
TO SING MY LOVE IN A CONCERTED MELODY,
IT'S NOT EASY TO EXPRESS MY OVERWHELMING HAPPINESS
IT'S JUST TOO GREAT, I GUESS, FOR SIMPLE WORDS TO SAY,

ACT I   DON'T BOTHER ME, I CAN'T COPE

BUT THE GREATEST THING ABOUT IT IS JUST
   KNOWING
THAT IT'S GROWING EVERY DAY.
   (GIRLS *cross* L.; MEN *enter* R. . . . STEVE, ROBERT, EDMUND.)
MY LOVE'S SO GOOD, MY LOVE'S SO FINE
HE MAKES ME FEEL SO GOOD, SO GLAD HE'S MINE

MY LOVE'S SO GOOD, MY LOVE'S SO FINE
HE MAKES ME FEEL SO GOOD, SO GLAD HE'S MINE
MY LOVE'S SO GOOD, MY LOVE'S SO FINE
HE MAKES ME FEEL SO GOOD, SO GLAD HE'S MINE

MY LOVE'S SO GOOD, MY LOVE'S SO FINE
HE MAKES ME FEEL SO GOOD, SO GLAD HE'S MINE
   CHARLAINE and GIRLS.
SHOW ME THAT SPECIAL GENE THAT SAYS I WAS BORN
   TO MAKE THE BEDS
SHOW ME THAT CERTAIN CHROMOSOME THAT SAYS
   MY PLACE IS IN THE HOME
MY PLACE IS IN THE HOME, MY PLACE IS IN THE HOME,
MY PLACE IS IN THE HOME.
   STEVE.
HIT IT, FELLAS!
   MALE DANCERS. (*While doing high kicks.*)
MY PLACE IS IN THE HOME
MY PLACE IS IN THE HOME
MY PLACE IS IN THE HOME.

BLACKOUT

No. 17: THEY KEEP COMING

(*The following dance is the glorification of "maleness."* THREE
   MALE DANCERS *cross* D. S. C. *and do variations of Black
   handshake.*)

   EDMUND, STEVE and ROBERT.
See that back?
See that hand?   } Dialogue no
          (*Turn* D. S.)   Music
You think we can tote a barge?
Well, we can.

STEVE.
And perform open heart surgery
  EDMUND.
And sit on the Supreme Court
  ROBERT.
And invent shoe-lasting machines.
  EDMUND.
And write books and plays
  STEVE.
And sing Verdi and Puccini
  (NAT *enters* U. R. *to* U. C.)
  NAT.
And become heavy-weight champion of the world.

} Dialogue no Music

INTERLUDE #1—*Repeat 11 times.*
THEY KEEP COMING
THEY KEEP COMING   } 2 bar vamp
THEY KEEP COMING

(ENTIRE CAST *enters, side-stepping.* SALOME, STEVE, JULIA, PAT *and* ROBERT *cross* L. *ladder.* NAT *crosses* C. AGNES, CHARLAINE, EDMUND *and* CLINTON *cross to* R. *ladder. They should be placed so voices come from different parts of stage.*)

  CLINTON.
YOU CAN STOP A ROSE FROM GROWING
IF YOU NIP IT IN THE BUD.
YOU CAN STOP A BROOK FROM FLOWING
BUT YOU CANNOT STOP A FLOOD.
  CHORUS.
THEY KEEP COMING . . .
THEY KEEP COMING . . .
  PAT.
FROM THE MISSISSIPPI DELTA
TO THE LOUISIANA BAYOU
COME THE GRANDSONS OF THE GRANDSONS
OF THE KINGS OF TIMBUKTU!
  CHORUS.
THEY KEEP COMING . . .
THEY KEEP COMING . . .

JULIA.
FROM THE MIDWESTERN STOCKYARDS
TO THE ARID WESTERN PLAINS
COME THE FREEDOM SEEKERS
AND THE BREAKERS OF THE CHAINS.
CHORUS.
THEY KEEP COMING ...
THEY KEEP COMING ...
NAT.
FROM THE IVIED HALLS OF HARVARD
STEVE.
AND THE DARK HALLWAYS OF HARLEM!
CHORUS.
THEY KEEP COMING ...
THEY KEEP COMING ...
AGNES.
SOME BY UNDERGROUND RAILROAD
ROBERT.
SOME BY DC SEVEN
SHEILA.
SOME BY MULE TRAIN
STEVE.
SOME BY CADILLAC.
CHORUS.
KEEP COMING ...
THEY KEEP COMING ...
(U. S. *cast crosses* D. S. *and* U. S.; D. S. *cast crosses* U. S. *and* D. S.)
RUNNING, WALKING, LIMPING, CRAWLING,
NEVER STOPPING ... JUST A COMING, COMING,
 COMING, COMING
COMING, COMING, COMING, COMING,
THEY KEEP COMING ...
THEY KEEP COMING ...
THEY KEEP COMING.
CHARLAINE.
WITH THEIR HUMOR AND THEIR LAUGHTER
AND THEIR RHYTHM AND THEIR BLUES,
WITH THEIR JAZZ AND GOSPEL
AND MANY VARIED HUES.

CHORUS.
THEY KEEP COMING . . .
THEY KEEP COMING . . .
JULIA.
WITH THEIR DUST MOPS
CLINTON.
AND THEIR TRACTORS
SALOME.
AND THEIR SOUL FOOD RECIPES
NAT.
WITH THEIR DISH RAGS
ROBERT.
AND THEIR HAMMERS
TIM.
AND THEIR PH D'S.
CHORUS.
THEY KEEP COMING . . .
THEY KEEP COMING . . .
THEY KEEP COMING . . .
THEY KEEP COMING . . .
THEY KEEP COMING . . .
(ALL *stop marching*.)
PAT.
THE NAT TURNERS
JULIA.
SOJOURNER TRUTHS
CLINTON.
THE JOHN BROWNS
NAT.
THE DUNBARS
STEVE.
AND THE WHEATLEYS
SALOME.
AND THE HANSBERRYS
AGNES.
AND THE HUGHES
CHARLAINE.
THE JACKIE ROBINSONS
TIM.
THE MEDGAR EVERS

JULIA.
THE SCHWERNERS
EDMUND.
THE GOODMANS
ROBERT.
THE CHANEYS
PAT.
THE JOHN AND BOBBY KENNEDYS
CHORUS.
KEEP COMING
SHEILA.
THE MALCOLMS
STEVE.
THE FRED HAMPTONS
NAT.
THE PAUL ROBESONS
CLINTON.
THE MARTIN LUTHER KINGS
CHORUS.
THEY KEEP (ALL *march*.)
COMING, COMING, COMING, COMING, COMING,
    COMING, COMING, COMING.
THEY KEEP COMING . . .
THEY KEEP COMING . . .
THEY KEEP COMING . . .
THEY KEEP COMING . . .

YOU CAN STOP A TRAIN FROM RUNNING

YOU CAN TURN A STREAM ASIDE

YOU CAN STOP AN ARMY COMING

BUT NO MAN CAN STOP THE TIDE.
        (ALL *move together* D. S. C.)
THEY KEEP COMING, COMING, COMING, COMING
    COMING, COMING, COMING, COMING,
        (ALL *move to original positions*.)
THEY KEEP COMING . . .
THEY KEEP COMING . . .

THEY KEEP COMING ...
THEY KEEP COMING ...
THEY KEEP COMING ...
THEY KEEP COMING ...
THEY KEEP COMING ...
THEY KEEP COMING ...

(ALL *stop*.)

No. 18: MY NAME IS MAN

(CLINTON *crosses* D. C.)

CLINTON.
I am my own cause
And my own effect
I've been around for centuries
And you don't know me yet.

(*Chord*. ALL *turn* C.)

WHEN MY FATHER SAW HIS SON
HE SAID, "I'M NAMING THIS ONE."
SO HE PONDERED HARD AND LONG,
AND IF YOU THINK THE NAME HE LAID ON ME WAS
    "RASTUS"
YOU'RE WRONG.

MY NAME IS "MAN."
LUSTY, BAD AND LOUD
STUBBORN, BLACK AND PROUD AS I WANNA BE.
JUST CALL ME "MAN"
AND I'VE JUST BEGUN
TO BE THE KIND OF ONE I'M GONNA BE.
I'M HEADED FOR PLACES
WHERE I'M OVERDUE,
SO GET OUT OF MY WAY BECAUSE I'M COMING
    THROUGH
LIKE A MAN.

WHEN MY MOTHER CALLED ME "BOY"
I WOULD ANSWER, "YES MA'AM,"
FOR I WAS A BOY THEN,

BUT SOME PEOPLE SEEM TO FORGET BOYS GROW UP TO
BE MEN.

JUST CALL ME "MAN"
WAKING UP AT LAST,
SHAKING OFF THE PAST AND HISTORY,
A BRAND-NEW MAN,
RESTLESS AND UPTIGHT,
NOT AFRAID TO FIGHT FOR MY WOMAN AND ME.

A MAN TAKES WHAT'S HIS
AND HE'S NOBODY'S CLOWN.
GONNA WALK THROUGH SOME DOORS OR I'M
    BREAKING THEM DOWN
LIKE A MAN.

SHUFFLING'S NOT MY WAY OF WALKING,
GRINNING'S NOT MY NATURAL LOOK,
GENUFLECTING'S NOT MY STYLE,
BUT YOU'LL GET TO KNOW ME 'CAUSE I'LL BE AROUND
    FOR A WHILE,
FOR A WHILE.

MY NAME IS "MAN"
THAT'S A PROPER NOUN,
BETTER WRITE IT DOWN SO YOU DON'T FORGET:
M-A-N, MAN.
IF YOU THINK I'M MEAN,
MISTER, YOU AIN'T SEEN A MEAN MAN YET.
I'M A CAT WHO DIGS LOVE,
BUT HOW MUCH CAN I GIVE
WHEN I'M FIGHTING AND DYING FOR MY RIGHT TO
    LIVE
LIKE A MAN?

MY NAME IS "MAN"
ARROGANT AND LOUD . . . STUBBORN BLACK AND
    PROUD AS I
WANNA BE.
IF YOU'RE A MAN
AND YOU'RE NOT AFRAID

BLACK AND WHITE, JOIN MY PARADE TO DIGNITY.
I'M MARCHING DOWN HIGHWAYS THAT HAVEN'T
  BEEN TROD,
DETERMINED TO LIVE TIL' I SHAKE HANDS WITH GOD
LIKE A MAN.

(*Music ends.*)

END OF ACT I

ACT TWO

No. 19: ALL I NEED

(SHEILA *enters* U. L., *crosses* D. C. COMPANY *enters* L. *and* R.)

SHEILA.
I DON'T NEED
    CHORUS.
    I DON'T NEED
SHEILA.
I DON'T NEED
    CHORUS.
    I DON'T NEED
SHEILA.
I DON'T NEED
    CHORUS.
    I DON'T NEED
SHEILA.
I DON'T NEED
    CHORUS.
    I DON'T NEED
SHEILA.
I DON'T NEED YOUR PLATITUDES
I DON'T NEED YOUR PITY
I DON'T NEED YOUR GALLUP POLLS
OR YOUR AD HOC COMMITTEE
I DON'T WANT YOUR SYMPATHY
WITHOUT RESPECT
I DON'T NEED YOUR STUDY GROUPS
OR YOUR BENIGN NEGLECT . . .
ALL I NEED
    CHORUS.
    ALL I NEED
SHEILA.
ALL I NEED
    CHORUS.
    ALL I NEED

SHEILA.
ALL I NEED
　CHORUS.
ALL I NEED
　SHEILA.
ALL I NEED
　CHORUS.
WHAT DO YOU NEED?
　　　　　　(CHORUS *leans forward*.)
　SHEILA.
I NEED
　CHORUS.
I NEED
　　　　　　(R. CHORUS *faces* D. S.)
　SHEILA.
I NEED
　CHORUS.
I NEED
　　　　　　(L. CHORUS *faces* D. S.)
　SHEILA.
LESS FAT BACK MORE GREEN BACK
AND YOU OFF MY BACK
I DON'T NEED
　CHORUS.
I DON'T NEED
　SHEILA.
I DON'T NEED
　CHORUS.
I DON'T NEED
　SHEILA.
I DON'T NEED
　CHORUS.
I DON'T NEED
　SHEILA.
I DON'T NEED
　CHORUS.
I DON'T NEED
　SHEILA.
I CAN'T USE A COURSE IN ETIQUETTE
WHEN MY RENT IS DUE
I DON'T NEED YOUR DR. JENSEN

TO STUDY MY I.Q.
I DON'T NEED YOUR THEORIES
FROM SOME BOOK YOU'VE READ
I DON'T NEED YOUR SOCIAL WORKER
PEEPING UNDER MY BED.
ALL I NEED
  CHORUS.
ALL I NEED
  SHEILA.
ALL I NEED
  CHORUS.
ALL I NEED
  SHEILA.
ALL I NEED
  CHORUS.
ALL I NEED
  SHEILA.
ALL I NEED

           (NAT *and* CLINTON *cross* C.)

  CHORUS.
WHAT DO YOU NEED?
  SHEILA.
I NEED
  CHORUS.
I NEED
  SHEILA.
I NEED
  CHORUS.
I NEED
  SHEILA.
LESS FAT BACK, MORE GREEN BACK
AND YOU OFF MY BACK
           (SHEILA *clear* U. S.)
  CLINTON.
I DON'T NEED
  CHORUS.
I DON'T NEED
  NAT.
I DON'T NEED
  CHORUS.
I DON'T NEED

CLINTON.
I DON'T NEED
CHORUS.
I DON'T NEED
NAT.
I DON'T NEED
CHORUS.
WHAT DO YOU NEED?
CLINTON.
I NEED
CHORUS.
I NEED
NAT.   } REPEAT
I NEED
CHORUS.
I NEED
CLINTON and NAT.
LESS FAT BACK, MORE GREEN BACK, AND YOU OFF
    MY BACK
    (*DANCE BREAK*; *repeat*; CLINTON, SHEILA, NAT *clear* U. S.)
SHEILA.
ALL I NEED
CHORUS.
ALL I NEED
SHEILA.
ALL I NEED
CHORUS.
ALL I NEED
SHEILA.
ALL I NEED
CHORUS.
ALL I NEED
SHEILA.
ALL I NEED
CHORUS.
WHAT DO YOU NEED?
SHEILA.
I NEED
CHORUS.
I NEED
I NEED LESS FAT BACK, MORE GREEN BACK,
AND YOU OFF MY BACK!

No. 20: QUESTIONS

(SALOME *crosses* D. L.; CHARLAINE *crosses* C.; S. L. GROUP *crosses* R. *and Ex.*, S. R. GROUP *crosses* L. *and Ex.*)

CHARLAINE.
SO MANY VOICES PREACHING
SO MANY HANDS KEEP REACHING
WHICH SOUND DO I LISTEN TO?
WHICH HAND DO I SHAKE?
QUESTIONS, QUESTIONS.

WITH EVERY DAY I'M FINDING
ANOTHER ROAD IS WINDING.
THERE'S A FORK IN EVERY ROAD
WHICH ONE DO I TAKE?

QUESTIONS, QUESTIONS,
KNOCKING ON THE DOORS OF MY MIND,
QUESTIONS, QUESTIONS,
AND SOMEWHERE THERE ARE ANSWERS I MUST FIND.

SO MANY TIMES I'VE WONDERED
WHERE WILL MY NAME BE NUMBERED?
WILL I STAND AMONG THE CROWD,
OR WILL I STAND ALONE?
QUESTIONS, QUESTIONS.

YES, I CAN HEAR YOU PREACHING.
AND I'VE STUDIED ALL YOUR TEACHING.
STILL, I KNOW THAT I MUST FIND
SOME ANSWERS OF MY OWN.

QUESTIONS, QUESTIONS,
KNOCKING ON THE DOORS OF MY MIND.
QUESTIONS, QUESTIONS,
AND SOMEWHERE THERE ARE ANSWERS I MUST FIND.

QUESTIONS, QUESTIONS,
KNOCKING ON THE DOORS OF MY MIND.
QUESTIONS, QUESTIONS,

AND SOMEWHERE THERE ARE ANSWERS I MUST FIND.
AND SOMEWHERE THERE ARE ANSWERS I MUST FIND.
(ALL *enter as* THEY *speak*.)
CHORUS.
Read your Bible, Sister!
All the news that's fit to print
Mohammed speaks
Crises
Ebony
TV Guide
Screw
Miss, Mrs., Miz.?
(CHORUS *laughs*.)
Violence begets violence begets violence begets violence.
Passiveness
Begets nothing, begets nothing, begets nothing.
Dixie Peach or Afro-Sheen?
Brotherhood, motherhood,
Red, White, and Blue!
Manhood, neighborhood,
Red, Black, and Green!
ALL.
Love, hate
Uptown, downtown
Separate state.
If I sit in I get arrested.
If I break in I get arrested.
If I shout nobody answers.
If I knock I'm Uncle Tom.
Questions!

(ALL *circle around* CHARLAINE C. S.; CHARLAINE *drops to her knees*.)

CHORUS.
Peace march. Poor march.
Freedom march. March, march.
Militant. Pacifist. Assimilator.
Moralist. Separatist. Agitator.
White Nigger. Black Nigger.
(ALL *peel off circle and Ex*. R. *and* L.)

Questions, questions, questions, questions,
Questions, questions, questions, questions . . .
   CHARLAINE.
AND SOMEWHERE THERE ARE ANSWERS I MUST FIND

No. 21:   IT TAKES A WHOLE LOT OF HUMAN FEELING

(CHARLAINE *sits* C. SALOME *crosses to* L. *ladder and sits.* SALOME
   hums, then sings.)

   SALOME.
IT TAKES A WHOLE LOT OF HUMAN FEELING
I KNOW FROM WHAT I'VE SEEN,
THAT IT TAKES A WHOLE LOT OF HUMAN FEELING
TO BE A HUMAN BEING.
  (*Spoken.*)
MISSISSIPPI BORN AND BRED
SOUTHERN FRIED FROM TOE TO HEAD,
NOW YOU LOOK AT MY BLACK FACE
AND WONDER WHY I LOVE THAT PLACE.

FRIEND, IT AIN'T NO MYSTERY.
THE LAND AIN'T DONE NO HARM TO ME,
IT JUST LAID THERE HOT AND DRIED
SOAKIN' UP THE TEARS I CRIED.

I DON'T HATE NO PIECE OF LAND
IT'S JUST SOME PEOPLE I CAN'T STAND,
DIRT'S JUST DIRT NO MATTER WHERE,
WHETHER HERE OR WHETHER THERE.

SOUTHERN DIRT DON'T BOTHER YOU
IT'S THE DIRT THAT PEOPLE DO,
BOSTON, LITTLE ROCK, IT'S ALL THE SAME,
MISSISSIPPI'S JUST A NAME.
   CHARLAINE.
MY MAMMA TAUGHT ME EARLY TO TURN THE OTHER
   CHEEK,
AND SHE MADE ME SWEAR TO THINK BEFORE I SPEAK.

SHE SAID, "THERE WILL BE TIMES YOU'LL THINK YOU
   HAVEN'T GOT A FRIEND,
BUT STAND UP TALL MY CHILD, AND DON'T YOU
   BEND."
BUT IT TAKES A WHOLE LOT OF HUMAN FEELING
I KNOW FROM WHAT I'VE SEEN,
THAT IT TAKES A LOT OF HUMAN FEELING
TO BE A HUMAN BEING.

THEY SAY OVERPOPULATION IS AN EVER-PRESENT
   THORN,
YET WE KILL EACH OTHER FAST AS WE ARE BORN.
AND SOMETIMES I HAVE TO WONDER WHAT STRANGE
   PLASM WE'RE MADE OF
WHEN WE HAVE TO ASK COMPUTERS WHOM TO LOVE.
IT TAKES A WHOLE LOT OF HUMAN FEELING,
I KNOW FROM WHAT I'VE SEEN,
THAT IT TAKES A LOT OF HUMAN FEELING
JUST TO BE A HUMAN BEING.

I OVERHEARD A MAN SAY
THAT HE WOULDN'T HURT A FLEA,
AND IF A FLY LIT ON HIS NOSE
HE'D LET IT BE.
WELL, MAYBE I'M JUST STUPID,
BUT IT'S HARD TO UNDERSTAND, THAT SAME MAN
   WOULDN'T EVEN SHAKE MY HAND.
   CHARLAINE and SALOME.
IT TAKES A WHOLE LOT OF HUMAN FEELING
I KNOW FROM WHAT I'VE SEEN,
THAT IT TAKES A WHOLE LOT OF HUMAN FEELING
TO BE A HUMAN BEING.

(CHARLAINE *rises, crosses to* SALOME, *forming mother and child
   impression. Hum, following verse once.*)

IT TAKES A WHOLE LOT OF HUMAN FEELING
TO BE A HUMAN BEING.
   (CHARLAINE *and* SALOME *cross* U. R. *and Ex. in fade out.*)

ACT II   DON'T BOTHER ME, I CAN'T COPE

No. 22:   MY LOVE'S SO GOOD (REPRISE)

(NAT, PAT, JULIA *enter* U. R. *to* R.)

NAT.
ANYTIME I'M FEELING BLUE THE ONLY THING I HAVE TO DO IS THINK OF HER (HIM)
AND WHEN I DO MY BLUES ARE GONE.
JUST THE MEMORY OF LAST NIGHT CAN GET THE MORNING STARTED RIGHT
AND KEEP MY EVERY HOUR BRIGHT FROM DAWN TO DAWN.

(NAT *crosses* C. GIRLS *cross* U. C.)

AND THE THOUGHT OF HAVING MORE OF WHAT I HAD THE NIGHT BEFORE CAN
MAKE MY SPIRITS SOAR ABOVE THE HIGHEST CLOUD,
THEN THE THOUGHT OF MY GOOD FORTUNE OVERTAKES ME AND
IT MAKES ME FEEL SO PROUD.

(NAT *crosses* U. C.)

MY LOVE'S SO GOOD. MY LOVE'S SO FINE.
SHE (HE) MAKES ME FEEL SO GOOD. SO GLAD SHE'S (HE'S) MINE.

(NAT *crosses* D. C.)

WHEN I WALK ALONG THE STREET I WANT TO STOP THE FOLKS
I MEET
AND TELL THEM JUST HOW
SWEET MY LOVE HAS BEEN TO ME.
WHEN I HEAR THE CHIRPING BIRDS I WANT TO FILL THEIR
MOUTHS WITH WORDS
TO SING MY LOVE IN A CONCERTED MELODY,
IT'S NOT EASY TO EXPRESS MY OVERWHELMING HAPPINESS
IT'S JUST TOO GREAT I GUESS FOR SIMPLE WORDS TO SAY.
BUT THE GREATEST THING ABOUT IT IS JUST KNOWING THAT IT'S GROWING EVERY DAY.

(GIRLS *cross* D. C. *to* NAT.)

MY LOVE'S SO GOOD. MY LOVE'S SO FINE

SHE (HE) MAKES ME FEEL SO GOOD. SO GLAD SHE'S
(HE'S) MINE.
    (NAT, PAT, JULIA *pose* F. S. *down.*)
CODA
MY LOVE'S SO GOOD. MY LOVE'S SO FINE
SHE (HE) MAKES ME FEEL SO GOOD. SO GLAD SHE'S
(HE'S) MINE.
    (F. S. *up again.*)

(EDMUND *and* STEVE *enter* L.; SALOME, ROBERT, AGNES, CHARLAINE *enter* R.)

NAT *and* CHORUS.
ANYTIME I'M FEELING BLUE THE ONLY THING I HAVE
 TO DO IS THINK OF YOU.
AND WHEN I DO MY BLUES ARE GONE.
JUST THE MEMORY OF LAST NIGHT CAN GET THE
 MORNING STARTED RIGHT
AND KEEP MY EVERY HOUR BRIGHT FROM DAWN TO
 DAWN.
AND THE THOUGHT OF HAVING MORE OF WHAT I HAD
 THE DAY BEFORE CAN
MAKE MY SPIRITS SOAR ABOVE THE HIGHEST CLOUD,
THEN THE THOUGHT OF MY GOOD FORTUNE OVERTAKES ME AND
IT MAKES ME FEEL SO PROUD.

MY LOVE'S SO GOOD. MY LOVE'S SO FINE
YOU MAKE ME FEEL SO GOOD. SO GLAD YOU'RE MINE.
    (ALL *stand, bend and clap. Freeze.*)

(CLINTON *enters* U. L. *with fans, crosses* D. C.; *hands fan to* NAT,
who counters around CLINTON *to* D. C. *and bows, then crosses*
U. S. ROBERT, SALOME, AGNES, JULIA, PAT, STEVE, CHARLAINE,
SHEILA, TIM *and* EDMUND *get fans.*)

   No. 23: GOOD VIBRATIONS
 NAT.
In a storefront church at eleven o'clock
Good vibrations make Sunday mornings rock.

CLINTON.
IN THE MORNING WHEN I WAKE,
IF I CAN SEE THE SUN, I GET
  CHORUS.
GOOD VIBRATIONS, GOOD VIBRATIONS
  CLINTON.
WHEN I GO TO BED AT NIGHT,
IF I KNOW MY JOB'S WELL DONE, I GET
  CHORUS.
GOOD VIBRATIONS, GOOD VIBRATIONS
  CLINTON.
EVERY TIME THAT I RECEIVE
AN ANSWER TO A PRAYER, I FEEL
  CHORUS.
GOOD VIBRATIONS, GOOD VIBRATIONS
  CLINTON.
JUST TO KNOW THAT THE ALMIGHTY POWER
IS STLL TURNED ON UP THERE GIVES ME
  CHORUS.
GOOD VIBRATIONS, GOOD VIBRATIONS
GOOD VIBRATIONS
  CLINTON.
ALL AROUND ME
  CHORUS.
GOOD VIBRATIONS
  CLINTON.
COMING TO ME
  CHORUS.
GOOD VIBRATIONS
  CLINTON.
I CAN FEEL THEM
  CHORUS.
GOOD VIBRATIONS
  CLINTON.
GOING THROUGH ME
WHEN I SEE YOU CLAP YOUR HANDS I FEEL
  CHORUS.
GOOD VIBRATIONS
  CLINTON.
WHEN I SEE YOU PAT YOUR FEET I FEEL

CHORUS.
GOOD VIBRATIONS
(ALL *pat feet*.)
CLINTON.
WHY DON'T YOU REACH OUT AND TOUCH YOUR NEIGHBOR'S HAND, DON'T YOU FEEL SOME GOOD VIBRATIONS
IF YOU FEEL THEM—YOU'LL UNDERSTAND WHAT I MEAN BY
CHORUS.
GOOD VIBRATIONS

CHORUS.	CLINTON.
GOOD VIBRATIONS	ALL AROUND ME
GOOD VIBRATIONS	I CAN FEEL THEM
GOOD VIBRATIONS	GOING THROUGH ME

CLINTON.
WHEN I SEE YOU CLAP YOUR HANDS I FEEL
CHORUS.
GOOD VIBRATIONS
CLINTON.
WHEN I SEE YOU TAP YOUR FEET I FEEL
CHORUS.
GOOD VIBRATIONS
CLINTON.
REACH OUT AND TOUCH YOUR NEIGHBOR'S HAND, DON'T YOU
FEEL SOME GOOD VIBRATIONS, IF YOU FEEL THEM YOU'LL UNDERSTAND WHAT I MEAN BY
CHORUS.
GOOD VIBRATIONS
GOOD VIBRATIONS (etc.) *Ad Lib Repeat*

(ROBERT *and* CHARLAINE *play tambourines* C. S.; SALOME *crosses* U. C. *and* D. S.—*shout*; SALOME *shout* D. R.—CLINTON *out of house*; CLINTON *shout, crosses* D. S., SALOME *clear* R.)

CHORUS.
GOOD VIBRATIONS (*Repeat Ad Lib*)
CHORUS.
GOOD VIBRATIONS (*Repeat Ad Lib*)
CLINTON.
GOING THROUGH ME

CHORUS.
GOOD, SO GOOD, GOOD, SO GOOD
GOOD VIBRATIONS.

No. 24: PRAYER

CLINTON.
Let us pray.
PAT. (*Sotto voce to the person next to her.*)
And then he said, "I'm interested in your soul."
CLINTON. (*Louder.*)
Let us pray.
JULIA. Oh, Lord, we come before You this morning with bowed heads and on bended knee, and we come mindful that the only bending and bowing You want us to do is in Thy holy presence.
AGNES. Amen.
JULIA. And, Lord, before I go on any further, I want to thank You in advance for everything we're about to ask You for. And, Lord . . .
CLINTON. Yes. (*To himself.*)
JULIA. (*Does a double take on hearing voice.*) Are you listening, Lord?
AGNES. He's listening, Sister.
STEVE. Lord? I want You to free me from temptation. When the numbers runner comes by. I want You to give me the will power to say, "Get thee behind me, numbers runner." But, just in case, Lord, You're on other business at the time, and I fall prey to my own human weakness, I ask that You fill all of my nights with dreams, dreams, dreams.
PAT. Lord, I ask You to protect me from the mugger. And in case the police department is not around to assist You at the time, Lord, I pray that when that mugger steps in my path, it's on the day *before* pay day.
JULIA. Before pay day.
PAT. And if he gets mad and vicious because I don't have a dollar in my pocketbook, and he proceeds to rough me up, I ask You to give me the strength to overcome him. That lacking, Lord, I beg You to invest me with the speed to run like h— . . .
SALOME. Help her, Jesus.
PAT. Now, I just want to ask a few more favors, Lord.

JULIA. Save some for next Sunday.

SALOME. Lord, I want to ask You to help me to hold my tongue when people call me out of my name because of what I am or am not. I want You to put soft words in my mouth, Lord, when the butcher or furniture man overcharges me. And when I'm carted off to jail because of what I believe in, I want You to keep me smiling all the while. And when they say I want too much too soon, all I ask is that You add fifty years to my life while I'm being patient. Now listen, Lord, are You listening?

AGNES. (*Impatiently.*) He's listening, Sister.

SALOME. I just want You to know one thing. Just in case . . . and I know You've got a lot of other problems, so just in case You can't manage to keep me reasonable and quiet and patient and forgiving and loving and smiling and above all, docile . . .

PAT. Docile, Lord, docile.

SALOME. I want You to know that it's all right, Lord, I understand. It's a lot to ask, even of You, Lord.

SERMON

CLINTON. I'm so glad
CHORUS. So glad
CLINTON. So glad
CHORUS. So glad
CLINTON. So glad
CHORUS. So glad
CLINTON. So glad
CHORUS. So glad
CLINTON. I'm so glad to see Sunday morning
CHORUS.
SO GLAD TO SEE SUNDAY MORNING
HMMMMMMMMM
    CLINTON. So glad
                        (CLINTON *crosses* D. C.)
CHORUS. So glad

(AGNES, PAT, STEVE, CHARLAINE, ROBERT *sit*. JULIA *crosses to* R. *ladder and sits*. NAT *and* EDMUND *sit atop ladders* R. *and* L.)

CLINTON. So glad

ACT II   DON'T BOTHER ME, I CAN'T COPE   55

    CHORUS. So glad
    CLINTON. So glad you could come, Sister.
           (CLINTON *to house, circle stage*.)
    CLINTON.
You can have Monday, Sister.
And you can have Tuesday, Brother.
You can have Wednesday
You can have Thursday
And you can have Friday
    JULIA. Friday? That's my day. (JULIA *begins to shout* C.)
    CLINTON. I'll even give you Saturday
    JULIA. Saturdays, too!
    CLINTON. Just give me Sunday.
    JULIA. Oooo—the whole weekend.
          (CLINTON *crosses to* JULIA *who is shouting*.)
    CLINTON. Because Sunday is a day of rest.
    JULIA. OOOOh, Preacher.
          (JULIA *collapses in* CLINTON's *arms*.)
    CLINTON. Sunday is the one day of the week when you can rest from all the battles you've had to fight all week long.
    JULIA. 666-9696.
    CLINTON. Praise the Lord!
          (JULIA *sits*. CLINTON *crosses* D. C.)
    CLINTON. Sunday is the one day of the week when you don't have to fight.
    SHEILA.
You,
You don't
You don't have
You don't have to
You don't have to
Fight!
          (CLINTON *crosses into house* D. L.)
    CLINTON. I say Sunday is the one day of the week when you don't have to fight. You don't have to fight the subway.
    CHORUS. Don't have to fight.
    CLINTON. You don't have to fight the supermarket.
    CHORUS. Don't have to fight.
    CLINTON. You don't have to fight with Charlie or Ann.
    CHORUS. Don't have to fight.
    CLINTON. Or the Infernal Revenue man.

CHORUS. Don't have to fight.
CLINTON. You don't have to fight the unemployment lines.
CHORUS. Don't have to fight.
CLINTON. The bus lines
CHORUS. Don't have to fight.
CLINTON. Or the picket lines.
CHORUS. Don't have to fight.

(CLINTON *onstage* D. R. *crosses* C.)

CLINTON. And one day
CHORUS. Don't have to fight.
CLINTON. One day.
CHORUS. Don't have to fight.
CLINTON. One day.
CHORUS. Don't have to fight.
CLINTON. Every day is going to be Sunday!
CHORUS. Hmmmmmm!
CLINTON. Thank God
CHORUS. Don't have to fight.
CLINTON. Thank God
CHORUS. Don't have to fight.
CLINTON. We won't have to fight.
CHORUS. Won't have to fight.
CLINTON. Won't have to fight.
CHORUS. Won't have to fight.
CLINTON. We won't have to fight.
CHORUS. Won't have to fight.
CLINTON. To keep from fighting!

(CLINTON *becomes increasingly pugnacious toward the end of the sermon.*)

No. 25: FIGHTING FOR PHARAOH

SALOME.
FIGHTING FOR PHARAOH, FIGHTING FOR CAESAR
FIGHTING FOR GOOD KING ARTHUR, FIGHTING FOR GLORY
FIGHTING FOR POWER, STATE OR RELIGION

CHORUS. (OOOOOOOOO etc. and vocal answers to soloist.)

FIGHTING FOR JURISDICTION AND
    TERRITORY
DYING FOR FREEDOM, DYING FOR
    SLAVERY,
DYING FOR COTTON AND FOR OIL
    AND GOLD
DYING FOR COUNTRY, DYING FOR
    HONOR
DYING FOR GOD AND PEACE AND
    BANNERS ON A POLE.

BEFORE WE LOSE OUR HUMANITY,
    LET'S STOP THIS INSANITY
AND TURN OUR CHILDREN'S
    HISTORY BOOKS AROUND
LET'S DO A LITTLE LIVING FOR PEACE,
NOT DYING, BUT LIVING FOR PEACE.
    (SALOME *crosses* D. C.)
NOW HISTORY'S PAGES SAY MAN
    THROUGH THE AGES
HAS NEVER RUN SHORT OF WAR.
FOR HE'S ALWAYS FOUND SOMETHING
WORTH FIGHTING AND KILLING
AND DYING FOR . . .

CHORUS.
(OOOOOOOOO
etc. and vocal
answers to
soloist.)

    (ALL *stand*, NAT *and* EDMUND *come down from ladders*.)
WELL, WE'VE BEEN
FIGHTING FOR PHARAOH
    CHORUS.
FIGHTING FOR PHARAOH
    SALOME.
FIGHTING FOR CAESAR
    CHORUS.
FIGHTING FOR CAESAR
    SALOME.   CHORUS.
FIGHTING FOR GOOD KING
    ARTHUR   OOH . . . etc.
FIGHTING FOR GLORY   OO - OO . . . etc.
FIGHTING FOR POWER   A STATE OF RELIGION
STATE OR RELIGION
    (SALOME *crosses* D. R.; S. R. GROUP *crosses* D. S. *of* S. L. GROUP.)
FIGHTING FOR JURISDICTION   OOOH . . . etc.

AND TERRITORY   OOOH . . . etc.
DYING FOR FREEDOM   DY-ING FOR
DYING FOR SLAVERY   DY-ING

(CHORUS *crosses* C. *forming two lines
facing* R.)

DYING FOR COTTON
AND FOR OIL AND GOLD   OO - OO
   (SALOME *crosses* U. R. *to* D. C.)
DYING FOR COUNTRY   DY-ING
DYING FOR HONOR   DY-ING
   (ALL *turn* D. S.)
DYING FOR GOD   DYING FOR GOD
AND PEACE AND BANNERS ON A POLE
BEFORE WE LOSE OUR HUMANITY, LET'S
   STOP THIS INSANITY
AND TURN OUR CHILDREN'S HISTORY
   BOOKS AROUND.
IT'S TIME TO TURN 'EM AROUND
              (SALOME *crosses* U. L. *to* D. C.)
LET'S DO A LITLE LIVING FOR PEACE
NOT DYING, BUT LIVING FOR PEACE
           (ALL *form a "V" with* SALOME *at apex*.)
IF EVERY MAN IN EVERY LAND
REACHED OUT HIS HAND IN UNDERSTANDING
WE COULD
   CHORUS.
DO A LITTLE LIVING
DO A LITTLE LIVING
DO A LITTLE LIVING IN PEACE

(*Cymbals creep in. As* SALOME *sings* ALL *touch her hand as* THEY
*leave the stage and go into audience to invite the audience to
"take your neighbor by the hand."*)

IF EVERY MAN IN EVERY LAND
REACHED OUT HIS HAND IN UNDERSTANDING
WE COULD
DO A LITTLE LIVING
DO A LITTLE LIVING
DO A LITTLE LIVING IN PEACE.

ACT II   DON'T BOTHER ME, I CAN'T COPE   59

   SALOME.
DO A LITTLE LIVING
DO A LITTLE LIVING
DO A LITTLE LIVING IN PEACE.
   (*Spoken.*)
If every man in every land would
We could

DO A LITTLE LIVING
DO A LITTLE LIVING
DO A LITTLE LIVING IN PEACE.
   CHORUS.
REACH
   SALOME.
REACH
   CHORUS.
REACH
   SALOME.
REACH
   CHORUS.
REACH
   SALOME.
OUT HIS HAND IN UNDERSTANDING
   CHORUS.   } *Chant*
REACH
   SALOME.
WE . . . WE . . . YOU . . . YOU . . .
YOU . . . ME EVERYBODY
         (SALOME *encourages those still seated.*)
   CHORUS.
EVERYBODY
   SALOME.
EVERYBODY
   CHORUS.
EVERYBODY
   SALOME.
WE COULD
   CHORUS.
DO A LITTLE LIVING
   SALOME.
WE COULD DO

CHORUS.
DO A LITTLE LIVING
   SALOME.
WE COULD DO
   CHORUS.
WE COULD DO A LITTLE LIVING IN PEACE
IN PEACE.

(ALL *cross on stage and crosses* S. L. *while* CHARLAINE *crosses* R. *During following 3 choruses* EDMUND *exits to change into original briefs.* ALL *remain with bowed heads as* SHE *sings.*)

   ALL and CHARLAINE.
IF EVERY MAN IN EVERY LAND REACHED OUT HIS
   HAND
IN UNDERSTANDING WE COULD
DO A LITTLE LIVING
DO A LITTLE LIVING
DO A LITTLE LIVING IN PEACE.

IF EVERY MAN IN EVERY LAND REACHED OUT HIS
   HAND
IN UNDERSTANDING WE COULD
DO A LITTLE LIVING
DO A LITTLE LIVING
DO A LITTLE LIVING IN PEACE.

IF EVERY MAN IN EVERY LAND REACHED OUT HIS
   HAND
IN UNDERSTANDING WE COULD
DO A LITTLE LIVING
DO A LITTLE LIVING
DO A LITTLE LIVING IN PEACE.

No. 26:   UNIVERSE IN MOURNING

   CHARLAINE.
A STORM IS RAGING IN THE WEST
THE TALLEST TREES ARE DYING
THE CLOUDS HAVE LOST THEIR FRIENDLINESS
AND ALL THE STARS ARE CRYING

THERE'S LIGHTING FLASHING IN THE EAST
WHERE ARMLESS HANDS ARE FLAILING
THE NEWBORN BABY'S TOOTHLESS MOUTH
IS STRETCHED IN CONSTANT WAILING, CONSTANT
   WAILING

WHILE SMOKE ENGULF'S THE NORTH AND SOUTH
WE DRINK AWAY THE TENSION
AND SIT AGAINST OUR PADLOCKED DOORS
WITH FEARS TOO GREAT TO MENTION

THE STOCK MARKET GOES DOWN AND UP,
WHICHEVER WAY THE WIND BLOWS,
WHILE THOSE WHO PRAY TO UNKNOWN GODS
PEEK OUT THROUGH WINDOWS, SHUTTERED
   WINDOWS

HAND IN HAND LET'S STAND AND JOIN
THE UNIVERSE IN MOURNING
STRAINING OUR VISIONS FOR A GLIMPSE
OF A NEW WORLD ABORNING, A NEW WORLD
   ABORNING

THERE'S THUNDER RUMBLING UNDERGROUND
WHERE HYDROGEN'S EXPLODING,
AND LAUGHTER HAS A STRANGE NEW SOUND
MIXED WITH A SOFT FOREBODING.

THE FRONT PAGE SHOWS THE FRIGHTENED FACE
OF A HIGH SCHOOL SOLDIER DYING,
HE GLADLY GAVE HIS LIFE THEY SAY,
I THINK SOMEONE IS LYING, SOMEONE'S LYING

SO HAND IN HAND WE STAND AND JOIN
THE UNIVERSE IN MOURNING
STRAINING OUR VISION FOR A GLIMPSE
OF A NEW WORLD ABORNING, A BRAND NEW WORLD
   ABORNING.

No. 27: WE'VE GOTTA KEEP MOVIN' (REPRISE)

CLINTON.
WE'VE GOTTA KEEP MOVIN', MOVIN', LORD
MOVIN', MOVIN', LORD
WE'RE A LONG WAY FROM WHERE WE'VE BEEN
BUT WE'VE GOTTA KEEP MOVIN' TIL WE MOVE ON IN.
              (CLINTON, SALOME *cross* R.)
SHEILA.
WE GOTTA KEEP PUSHIN', PUSHIN', LORD
PUSHIN', PUSHIN', LORD
WE'VE PUSHED A LONG WAY FROM WHERE WE'VE BEEN
BUT WE GOTTA KEEP PUSHIN' TIL WE PUSH ON IN.
              (EDMUND *enters* U. R.; *Dance* C.)
CHARLAINE.
WE'VE GOTTA KEEP RUNNIN', RUNNIN', LORD
RUNNIN', RUNNIN', LORD
WE'VE RUN A LONG WAY FROM WHERE WE'VE BEEN
BUT WE'VE GOTTA KEEP RUNNIN' TIL WE RUN ON IN.
ALL.
WE'VE GOTTA KEEP MOVIN', MOVIN', LORD
MOVIN', MOVIN', LORD
WE'RE A LONG WAY FROM WHERE WE'VE BEEN,
BUT WE'VE GOTTA KEEP MOVIN' TIL WE MOVE ON IN.

No. 28: GOOD VIBRATIONS (REPRISE)

(Final Bows)

WE'RE SO GLAD YOU CAME TO SEE US
AND WE WANT YOU ALL TO KNOW
WE'VE HAD SOME

GOOD VIBRATIONS, GOOD VIBRATIONS

NOW WE HAVE TO LEAVE YOU,
BUT JUST BEFORE WE GO
LET'S HAVE SOME MORE

GOOD VIBRATIONS, GOOD VIBRATIONS

EVERYBODY HERE COME ON AND JOIN US IN THIS
  SONG
IF YOU'RE FEELING

GOOD VIBRATIONS, GOOD VIBRATIONS

AND WHEN YOU WALK OUT THAT DOOR,
WE HOPE YOU'LL TAKE ALONG
A LOT OF GOOD,

GOOD VIBRATIONS, GOOD VIBRATIONS

GOOD VIBRATIONS, GOOD VIBRATIONS.
   (ALL *continue singing "Good Vibrations" through their exit.*)

PROPERTY LIST

Fans for each member of the cast.
Fans to be distributed to the audience (the number of fans is left to the discretion of director or budget of production).

COSTUME PLOT

Contemporary American clothes.
No costumes

NOTES ON THE PRODUCTION

This entertainment can be done with a minimum cast of nine. To insure sufficient body to the music and credibility to "the history of the dance" it is suggested that you use eight dancers and ten singers including principals. As the piece is the thing caution must be taken not to over-produce it. Two ladders (8' and 6', S. R. and S. L.), a scrim hiding the orchestra U. S. C. on a platform should be sufficient. This suggestion, however, is not meant to inhibit a designer who might conjure up an entirely new way of dressing the playing area.

Extreme care must be taken to insure that this is a "hymn to us." Black pride and dignity must be stressed so that "tongue in cheek" sequences read the way they were written rather than minstrel turns. When we say "you think we got rhythm we got a lot" we do a tap or a dance traditionally credited to Black people, but it must be done with joy and respect. The dancer must then do a solo that shows his universal artistry—the artist who has conquered the technique and skill that enables him to compete in the multiracial world.

Because we are dealing with so many universal truths, the director should not be trapped into thinking that the piece is simpler than it, in fact, is. It must be philosophical without being ponderous, it must never be patronizing, it must illuminate the White audience and bring pride and honor and identification to the Blacks. Because the lyrics forward the piece, they must be clearly sung. There is music in the poetry, so it must be rendered with all that "sense of rhythm of which we are so proud."

Above all it must be done with taste, affection, and the realization that two Black women wanted young Black artists to have material on which to sharpen their instruments and watch as their grandparents sit in the audience and say "Amen."

Vinnette Carroll
April 1976

LADDERS

Orchestra

scrim

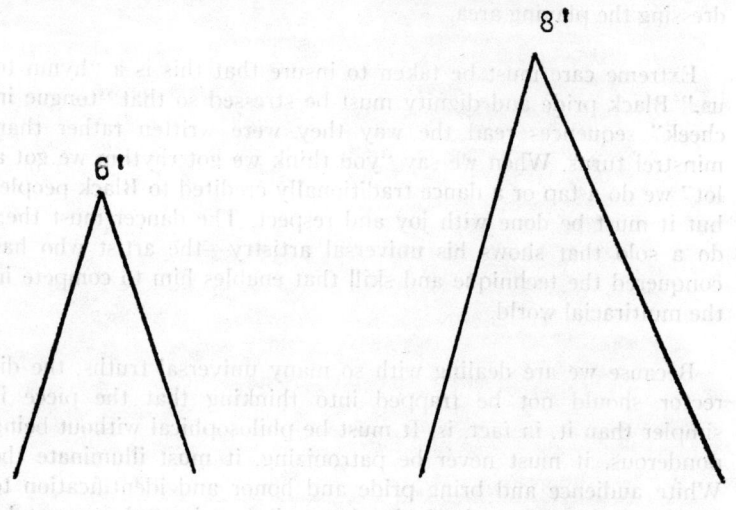

These are ordinary double-rung ladders bought from a hardware store and painted grey.

DON'T DRINK THE WATER

By WOODY ALLEN

FARCE

12 men, 4 women—Interior

A CASCADE OF COMEDY FROM ONE OF OUR FUNNIEST CO-MEDIANS, and a solid hit on Broadway, this affair takes place inside an American embassy behind the Iron Curtain. An American tourist, caterer by trade, and his family of wife and daughter rush into the embassy two steps ahead of the police, who suspect them of spying and picture-taking. But it's not much of a refuge, for the ambassador is absent and his son, now in charge, has been expelled from a dozen countries and the whole continent of Africa. Nevertheless, they carefully and frantically plot their escape, and the ambassador's son and the caterer's daughter even have time to fall in love. "Because Mr. Allen is a working comedian himself, a number of the lines are perfectly agreeable . . . and there's quite a delectable bit of business laid out by the author and manically elaborated by the actor. . . . The gag is pleasantly outrageous and impeccably performed."—*N. Y. Times.* "Moved the audience to great laughter. . . . Allen's imagination is daffy, his sense of the ridiculous is keen and gags snap, crackle and pop."—*N. Y. Daily News.* "It's filled with funny lines. . . . A master of bright and hilarious dialogue."—*N. Y. Post.*

(Slightly restricted. Royalty, $50-$25, where available.)

THE ODD COUPLE

By NEIL SIMON

COMEDY

6 men, 2 women—Interior

NEIL SIMON'S THIRD SUCCESS in a row begins with a group of the boys assembled for cards in the apartment of a divorced fellow, and if the mess of the place is any indication, it's no wonder that his wife left him. Late to arrive is another fellow who, they learn, has just been separated from his wife. Since he is very meticulous and tense, they fear he might commit suicide, and so go about locking all the windows. When he arrives, he is scarcely allowed to go to the bathroom alone. As life would have it, the slob bachelor and the meticulous fellow decide to bunk together—with hilarious results. The patterns of their own disastrous marriages begin to reappear in this arrangement; and so this too must end. "The richest comedy Simon has written and purest gold for any theatregoer. . . . This glorious play."—*N. Y. World-Telegram & Sun.* "His skill is not only great but constantly growing. . . . There is scarcely a moment that is not hilarious."—*N. Y. Times.*

(Royalty, $50-$35.)

THE SENTIMENTAL SCARECROW
(ALL GROUPS)

MUSICAL-COMEDY-FANTASY—1 ACT
Book and Lyrics by S. Charles Shertzer
and Music by Nathan Brown

A musical version of Rachel Field's "The Sentimental Scarecrow." 2 men, 5 females, and a band of gypsies. (Exterior) Modern Costumes. 5 songs, incidental music, and a gypsy dance.

The Scarecrow is exactly what the title suggests; he wishes to become a human; in order to realize his wish, he must convince some young lady to not only kiss him, but to agree to marry him. The fun of this production is found in the Scarecrow's antics as he attempts to win a wife. The music and the lyrics are delightfully amusing, plus exciting, and at times filled with genuine pathos.

The songs include "Half the Day's Gone," "A Cold Stare and a Withering Glance," "Gypsy Caravan," "I've Got to Have a Dame," and "Funny Looking."

Music on rental and deposit, write for information.

Royalty, $15-$10.

A Pink Party Dress

MUSICAL—1 ACT
David Rogers and Mark Bucci

A musical version of Margaret Bland's "Pink and Patches." 1 man, 3 females. (Exterior) Modern Costumes. 5 songs. 35 minutes.

The story of Texie, a mountain girl who hopes to escape the life of hardship and poverty her mother and other mountain women lead. She longs for the richer life she has observed at a fashionable hotel nearby and for a pink party dress instead of the patched brown denim she is forced to wear. Then a visitor to the hotel offers to give Texie a dress. Whether her proud mother will allow her to accept it and whether it will be the Pink Party Dress form the story of this charming folk musical.

The songs include "Women Folk Work Fer Men Folk," "A Pink Party Dress," "Lovely Evening, Isn't It?," and others. Complete libretto and piano score.

Royalty, $15.00 first performance
$10.00 each additional performance.